Huntingdon Area
Middle School Library
Huntingdon, Pa.

Class No. *599.32*

Acc. No. *13520*

THE BEAVER

BY
JEROLYN ANN NENTL

EDITED BY
DR. HOWARD SCHROEDER
Professor in Reading and Language Arts
Dept. of Elementary Education
Mankato State University

PRODUCED AND DESIGNED BY
BAKER STREET PRODUCTIONS
Mankato, MN

CRESTWOOD HOUSE
Mankato, Minnesota

LIBRARY OF CONGRESS CATALOGING IN PUBLICATION DATA

Nentl, Jerolyn Ann.
  The beaver.

  (Wildlife, habits, and habitat)
  SUMMARY: Describes the physical characteristics, behavior, and natural environment of the beaver.
  1. Beavers—Juvenile literature. [1. Beavers] I. Schroeder, Howard. II. Title. III. Series.
  QL737.R632N46   1983   599.32'32   83-5323
  ISBN 0-89696-219-4

International Standard Book Number:	Library of Congress Catalog Card Number:
Library Binding 0-89696-219-4	83-5323

ILLUSTRATION CREDITS:

Steve Kuchera: Cover
Lynn Rogers: 5, 9, 10, 13, 14, 16, 20, 24, 27, 29, 30, 32, 34, 37, 41, 43
Bob Williams: 6, 22, 38-39
Steve Durst: 19
U.S. Forest Service: 44

13520

Copyright© 1983 by Crestwood House, Inc. All rights reserved. No part of this book may be reproduced in any form without written permission from the publisher, except for brief passages included in a review. Printed in the United States of America.

Hwy. 66 South, Box 3427
Mankato, MN 56002-3427

TABLE OF CONTENTS

Introduction: 4

Chapter One: What beavers look like 8
    A hard-working animal
    Plump and stocky
    Fur in two layers
    Front teeth like chisels
    A tail like a paddle
    At home in the water

Chapter Two: Where beavers live 17
    At home in the North
    A fresh-water animal

Chapter Three: The life of a beaver 21
    Eats only plants
    Finding a mate
    Raising the kits
    Predators

Chapter Four: The beaver at work 31
    Working in pairs
    Lodges
    Dams
    Canals

Chapter Five: The future of the beaver 41
    Controls are needed

Map: 45

Index/Glossary 47

INTRODUCTION:

All is silent as the sun sinks behind the hills. The sky to the west is streaked with the blues, pinks and grays of the last bit of daylight. The forest is quiet in the growing darkness. Not a breeze ripples the water of a pond at the edge of the trees.

Suddenly a small nose appears just above the surface of the water, sniffing for signs of danger. Then a head appears. The animal silently swims around the pond, making sure all is safe. Once it is satisfied that there is no danger lurking in the shadows, it walks ashore. Using its wide, flat tail as a prop, it sits up on its hind legs. It shakes its head a bit and scratches its big belly. Then it settles down to groom its beautiful brown fur. When it is finished, it walks over to a small tree and starts to cut it down with its large front teeth.

This big furry animal that cuts down trees is the beaver. It is a rodent, an animal that gnaws or chews on things. The beaver is the largest rodent in the Northern Hemisphere and the second largest rodent in the world. Only the capybara of South America is larger.

Today's beaver is the descendent of beavers called *Castoroides* that lived thousands of years ago. These giants weighed up to eight hundred pounds. Most of them died during the ice age when sheets of ice moved down from the far north and covered the land. Scientists believe that a few of these giants must have survived. Through the years these survivors changed very little except for their size. Now they are much smaller.

At the time the white man came, there were at least sixty million beavers in North America.

Beavers played a unique role in the history of North America. Much of the continent was first

The "business end" of a beaver — *its large front teeth*.

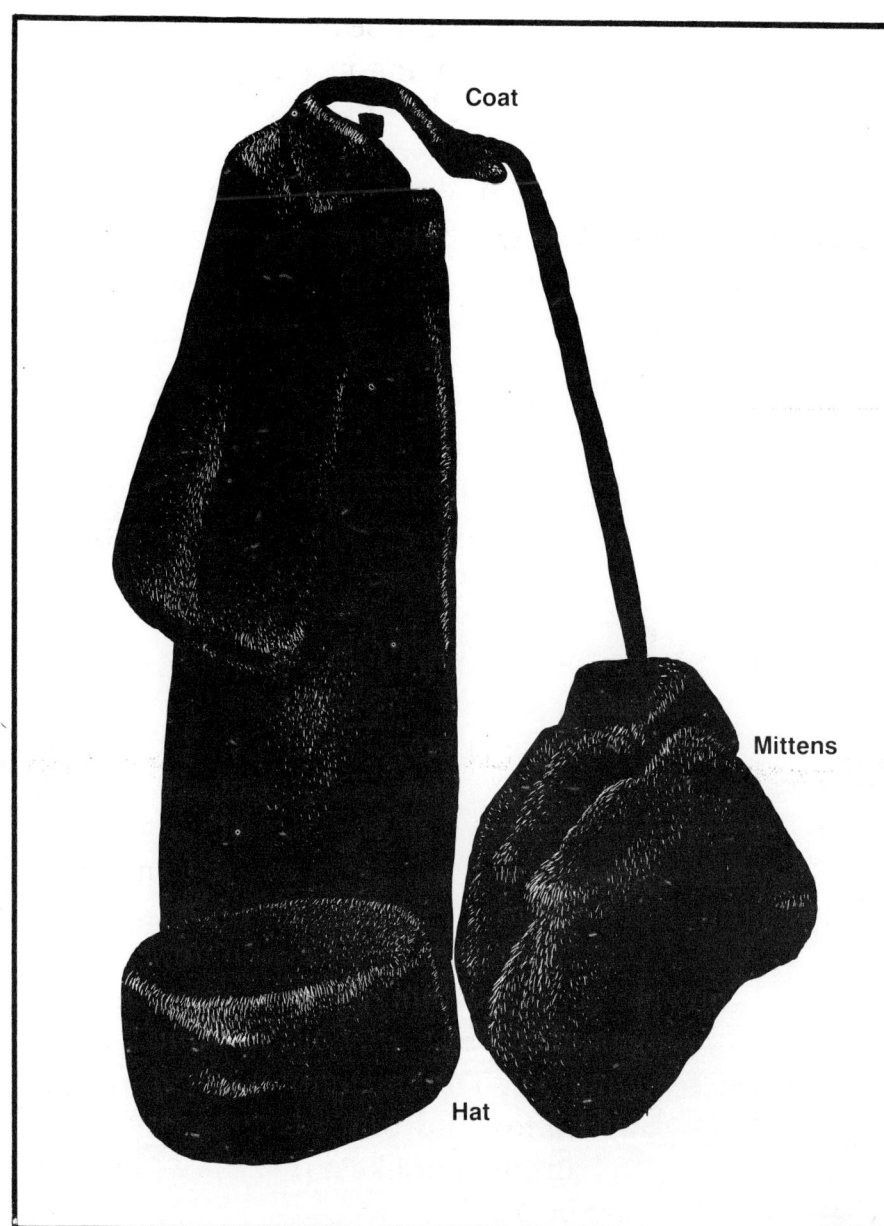

Some examples of clothing made from beaver fur.

explored by trappers seeking beaver fur. This fur was prized in Europe for making men's hats and trimming women's clothing. Fur traders would come to America to exchange either money or goods for beaver fur, or pelts. A good pelt was worth several dollars. Four pelts would buy a blanket and twelve would buy a rifle. Most trappers could take several beavers a day throughout a season. The more beavers a trapper could get, the richer he could become. At one time beaver fur was so valuable it was called "brown gold." For more than two hundred years, companies sent beaver fur to Europe in large quantities. The Hudson Bay Company alone shipped three million pelts to London from 1853 to 1877.

The places where trappers and traders met to buy and sell the pelts became known as trading posts. These trading posts soon became army posts. Then towns grew up around the army posts. The trails that fur trappers blazed were the routes that early settlers followed to the West. Some fur trappers became guides for the settlers, leading their wagon trains across the continent.

Beaver trapping was one of the things that brought white men into conflict with the American Indians. The Indians had held the beaver in great respect for centuries. They hunted it for food, using the pelts for clothing and bed robes to keep them warm. The Indians did not like it that the white men killed so many beavers.

CHAPTER ONE:

A hard-working animal

The beaver is an easy animal to identify, with its big front teeth and wide, flat tail. Other rodents also have big front teeth, but no other animal has such a tail.

The beaver is a hard-working animal and is known all over the world for the dams it builds. It builds them to make sure there will always be plenty of deep water in which it can safely live. A beaver feels truly safe only in the water of its home pond.

A beaver does not hibernate. It is active all year, although it spends most of the winter snug in its lodge or burrow. The beaver feeds, works, and plays mostly in the late afternoon or at night. Scientists call this way of living crepuscular or nocturnal.

The beaver did not always live this way. Writers of long ago told of beavers that worked and played during the day. The beaver perhaps sensed that it was being hunted. As people began to move onto its homeland, it began to use darkness to help protect itself.

Today, deep in the safety of the woods, hikers and

This photo shows a beaver dam, and the pond it formed.

campers sometimes still see a pond with beavers working and playing in the sunlight.

Plump and stocky

A beaver is a plump, stocky animal with a highly humped back. Its neck is short and thick and very flexible. It has a large skull, for a rodent, and large, powerful jaws. Its sense of hearing and smell are very sharp. For a rodent, the beaver has a highly developed brain.

A beaver's hind legs are strong and longer than its forelegs. This is why its back is humped. The beaver's hind feet are very large, but its forefeet are quite small. Each of its four feet has five toes with long, stout nails called claws. The toes on its hind feet are webbed, but those on its forefeet are not. The second claw from the outside on each hind foot is cleft, or split. This double claw is used for combing its fur. A beaver's forefeet are so flexible that it can use them almost as well as a human uses its hands.

Its webbed, hind foot makes the beaver a good swimmer.

Fur in two layers

A beaver's fur is in two layers: an undercoat and an outcoat. The gray fur of the undercoat is soft and short, very fine, and thickly curled. The outercoat is made up of long, shiny guard hairs that are coarse and bristly. These guard hairs protect the underfur. The color of the outercoat varies from dark brown to tan. On the beaver's back it is mostly a rich, glossy brown. Sometimes it has a hint of rust or chestnut color. Often times it is tan, almost yellow. The beaver's belly is a pale brown.

A beaver spends much of the time grooming its coat with the built-in combs on its hind feet. This grooming takes out the tangles and removes ectoparasites such as lice and fleas. A beaver waterproofs its fur by coating it with oil. This oil comes from one of two pairs of glands near the base of the beaver's tail.

The second pair of glands are scent glands called castors. These glands produce a substance called castoreum. For centuries, castoreum was used as a cure-all medicine. People used it to combat almost anything that ailed them. It was used as bait for the beaver traps, too. When a trapper took a beaver's pelt, he also took its castor glands.

A beaver's coat is at its fullest, or prime, by the early part of each year. Then in late spring or summer, the beaver slowly molts or loses these hairs. It begins growing a new fur coat for the next winter. This is nature's way of keeping furry animals warm in winter and cool in summer. If it did not molt its heavy winter coat, the beaver would be much too hot during the summer months.

Front teeth like chisels

Like other rodents, a beaver has two large front teeth called incisors. These teeth are bright orange. As a beaver gnaws, the lower pair of incisors works against the upper pair. This gives them a very sharp edge, just like a chisel.

A beaver's incisors never stop growing. They grow in an arc, with their roots deep inside the skull. If a beaver does not gnaw, the incisors may grow into a complete circle. They may even pierce the beaver's jaw or skull, causing its death.

Behind a beaver's incisors there are eight more cheek teeth called molars that are not ever-growing. These are used for grinding whatever the beaver eats.

Between a beaver's incisors and its cheek teeth is a very large empty space. This provides a place where the beaver can easily carry large branches and logs.

A beaver carries sticks in the empty space between its incisors and its cheek teeth.

A tail like a paddle

A beaver's wide, flat tail is unique. In a large adult beaver, it may be twelve to eighteen inches (31-46 cm) long from base to tip. It is six or seven inches (15-18 cm) wide, but less than an inch (2.5cm) thick. It is shaped like a paddle and is very powerful. The base of a beaver's tail is covered with the same fur that covers its body. The flattened part of the tail,

A beaver's tail is covered with scales.

which is eight to twelve inches (21-31 cm) long, has no fur. It has scales like a fish or a reptile plus a few short bristly hairs.

    A beaver's tail is used as a rudder, helping it steer through the water. This is most important when a beaver is carrying a heavy branch in its mouth. To overcome the pull of the branch, the beaver turns its tail in the opposite direction. This allows it to steer a straight course.

At home in the water

A beaver spends much of its time in the water, and is an excellent swimmer and diver. As a rule, a beaver swims at a speed of about two miles an hour. When chased it can reach a speed of six miles an hour. A beaver pushes itself through the water with its large hind feet, spreading its webbed toes. It strokes first with one foot and then the other. A beaver does not use its forefeet while swimming. It carries them balled up like fists against its chest. It often uses them to push aside sticks or other things that get in its way.

A beaver also has watertight valves in its ears and nose. These valves close when it dives under the water. Clear eyelids also slide across its eyes to protect them while the beaver is underwater. These clear eyelids are called nictitating membranes.

Two furry flaps of skin close off the beaver's mouth behind its incisors. This allows it to gnaw on wood while underwater without getting water in its mouth. These same flaps help keep wood chips out of its mouth while it is felling trees on land.

As a rule, a beaver stays underwater for only two or three minutes. It can last up to fifteen minutes if it must. A beaver can swim underwater for up to half a mile (.8 km). Such feats are possible because a beaver's heartbeat and circulation rate slow as it dives. When its heart beats slower, a beaver needs less oxygen.

A beaver is far less at home on land. Its big webbed feet make it slow and clumsy. It tires easily because of its large size, and it is not a good climber. All this makes the beaver an easy prey for predators while it is on land. If it is chased, a beaver can gallop but only for a short distance. A beaver is much safer in the water.

The beaver is clumsy on land, and doesn't like to get too far from water.

CHAPTER TWO:

At one time the beaver was found in the forests of all the Northern Hemisphere. In the Old World of Europe and Asia it was called the European Beaver, *Castor fiber*. In the New World of Canada and the United States it was called the American Beaver, *Castor canadensis*. These two species, or kinds, of beaver are very much alike. They differ only in the shape of their skull.

At home in the North

The European Beaver lived from Scandinavia south to the Mediterranean Sea, from the British Isles east to Siberia. The American Beaver lived across Alaska and Canada south to the Rio Grande River. The only places this beaver did not live was in the Arctic tundra, the deserts of the southwest, and the Florida Peninsula. At one time, there were twenty-four varieties, or subspecies, of American Beaver.

The beaver's wide range ended because of people's greed for beaver fur and castoreum. So many beavers had been trapped that the animal was extinct in most of Europe by the nineteenth century. It is now found only in a few places in central Europe. The beaver lasted a little longer in North America. Yet by the twentieth century it was almost extinct on this continent, too.

Early in this century, laws were passed in both the United States and Canada to protect the beaver. These laws made beaver trapping illegal in some places.

Wildlife managers then began the job of restocking areas where the beaver had been trapped out. They did this first by live-trapping pairs of beaver mates from some of the few places where colonies still existed. Then they transported them to places where beavers had been trapped out and released them. The beavers thrived, just as beavers had done for centuries before the trappers came. This was possible because of their low natural death rate and steady reproduction rate. In most places in North America there are now plenty of beavers. Trapping is allowed again in most places, too, but now it is controlled.

A fresh-water animal

All beavers live in fresh water. They prefer the wilderness where they will be left alone. If such a place cannot be found, beavers will settle close to a city or town.

Most beavers prefer small lakes and slow-moving streams. Some also live along the edges of large lakes and fast-moving rivers. Beavers that live along these larger, faster-moving waters dig homes in the banks called burrows. They are often called bank beavers. Those that live along the slower streams build homes called lodges in the middle of the water. Both kinds of beavers also dig a series of smaller holes along the banks. These are called refuge holes. They are used by the beavers as resting spots and hiding places.

This lodge is in a lake. Beavers that live in lakes don't need to build dams.

Wherever beavers live, they want water that is deep enough to hide the entrances to their burrows, lodges and refuge holes. They also want deep water so that it does not freeze solid in winter. If it did, they would become prisoners. They might starve to death before spring. Deep water helps protect the beavers from predators, too. It is also a place where they can store food for the winter.

This is why many beavers build dams. The dams back up the water, making it deeper.

A beaver heads for the underwater entrance to its lodge.

CHAPTER THREE:

Beavers are very sociable animals. Scientists call this kind of animal gregarious. As a rule, three generations of beavers live together in a close-knit family called a colony. There are the parent beavers, the new-born beavers of that year, which are called kits, and kits of the previous year. These older kits are called yearlings. On a large lake or pond, there may be more than one beaver colony, if there are enough food trees in the area.

Muskrats sometimes make their homes in the sides of large beaver lodges. Many other smaller animals make the beaver ponds and meadows their homes, too. So do fish, birds, and many insects. Moose and deer drink and feed at beaver ponds. None of this bothers the beavers.

Eats only plants

The beaver is a strict vegetarian. Scientists call these animals who eat only plants herbivorous.

The main food for a beaver is the soft bark of trees. A beaver will often sit up on its hind legs and feed on a branch or a log corn-on-the-cob style!

Beavers especially like the tender inner bark, or cambium, of the tree. This is the layer between the outside bark and the inner core of wood. Beavers also eat a tree's leaves, buds, and roots. They will eat saplings, twigs, and small branches completely. They will eat only the bark and cambium of the larger branches and main tree trunk. They use what remains of these pieces when building their dams and lodges.

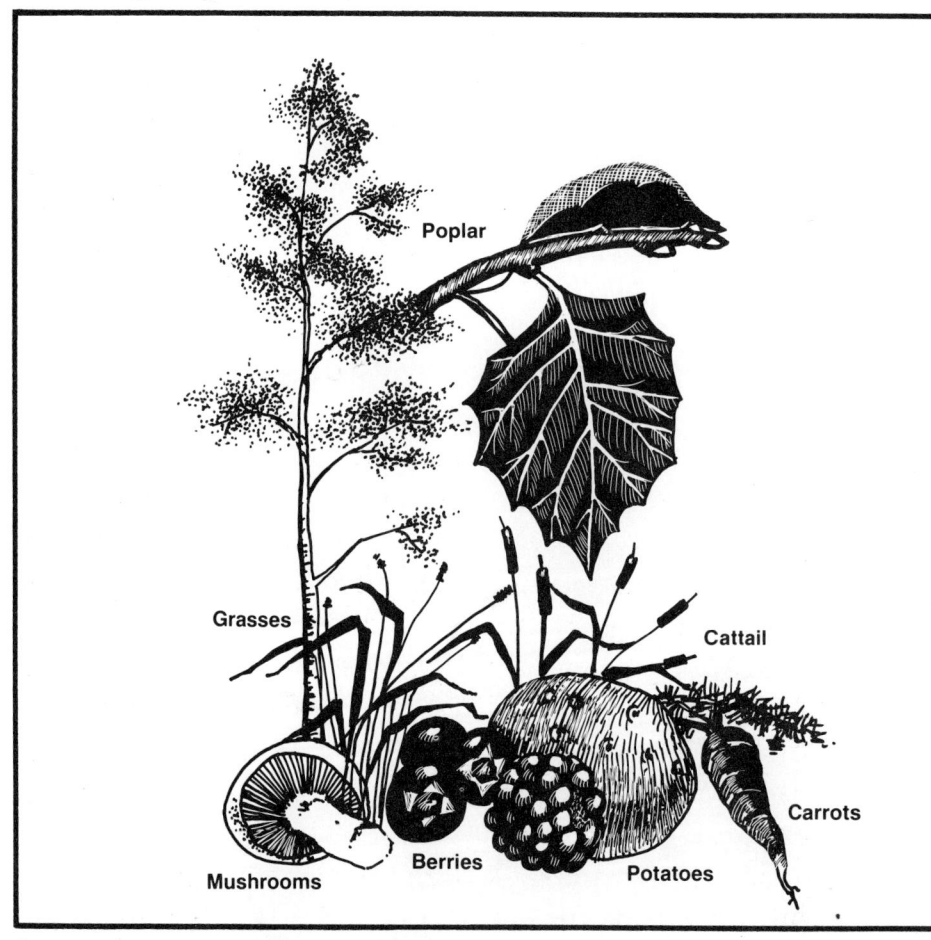

Some of the beaver's favorite foods.

Aspen, or poplar, is a beaver's favorite food tree. If there are none of these, it will feed on other trees such as cottonwood, willow, birch and alder. Beavers also like the loblolly pine, sweet gum and sweet bay trees that grow in the South.

Trees are only part of what the beavers eat. They also eat grasses, ferns, berries and mushrooms. They especially like waterplants such as cattails, water lilies, bulrushes, duckweed and pondweed. They feed on the green scum that forms on their ponds, too. Beavers will feed on clover and alfalfa. They also like vegetables such as carrots, turnips and potatoes. Beavers like apples, too. In places where there are farms, gardens, or orchards, beavers can do a lot of damage!

Exactly what a beaver eats depends on where he lives and the time of the year.

Beavers that live in colder climates spend the winter in their lodges or burrows on ice-covered ponds. To survive, they must have stored enough food to last until spring. To do this, a beaver anchors branches, twigs, and sticks into the mud at the bottom of its pond. These underwater food piles are called winter food caches. When a beaver gets hungry, it swims beneath the ice to the winter food cache. It takes a branch or a log back to the lodge to eat.

A beaver can easily swim around beneath the ice, but it cannot survive in the cold water for too long.

This beaver is adding branches to its winter food cache.

The water level of a pond often drops a little after the surface freezes. When this happens there is a thin layer of air between the water and the ice on top. When a beaver needs to breathe, it swims up to the ice and sticks its nose into this layer of air. It can also stop by one of its refuge holes for a fresh breath of air.

Beavers living in warmer climates do not make winter food caches. It does not get cold enough in these places to freeze the water where they live. These beavers also do not cut down as many trees as do beavers living in the colder climates. They feed more off the other kinds of plants that grow all year in the warm weather.

Finding a mate

Beavers leave their parents in the spring when they are two years old. It is time for each to seek a mate of its own and a place to build its own colony. A young beaver may wander only a few miles from its parents' home. Some may go as far as fifty miles.

A beaver finds a mate with the help of scent mounds. These mounds are sometimes called mud patties. They are piles of mud, grass, leaves and sticks about one foot high (31 cm). On these piles a beaver deposits some of its castoreum. The odor of the castoreum can be smelled by other beavers over a long distance. The other beavers can tell by this smell if it was a male or female who made the scent mound. The smell will often attract unmated beavers of the opposite sex.

Once a beaver has found its mate, it usually stays

with that mate until it dies. Scientists call animals that mate for life monogamous. There are only a few such animals in the world.

Scent mounds mark the boundaries of a beaver's territory. Male and female scent mounds in the same territory tell other beavers that a mated pair of beavers lives there. Beaver mates want to be left alone to build their colony. The male mate will attack any male beaver who ignores his scent mounds and comes too close to the home pond. The female mate will attack any females who cross the boundaries. This is one of the times that the beaver will start a fight.

The beaver pair does not breed until January or February. The female beaver carries her young within her for about four months. This time is called the gestation period. The young kits are born in April or May.

The beaver family is a close-knit one. Life centers on the mother beaver. Such a family life is called matriarchal by scientists.

Raising the kits

Beaver kits are born covered with soft fur and with their eyes open. Their incisor teeth show even at birth. A kit is about one foot (31 cm) long and weighs about a pound (.5 kg) or less. It is able to follow its mother in the water on the day it's born.

As a rule there are three or four kits in a litter, but there may be as many as eight. Yet a mother beaver has only four nipples with which to feed her milk to her young ones. So if there are more than four kits, they must take turns nursing. Once the family is well-fed and content, the kits often coo softly. If they are still hungry, they can sometimes be heard whining.

Within a week, the kits have become good swimmers. They play in the water, chasing each other back and forth. Much of their time is spent watching their parents work. By the time they are several weeks old, they are following their mother on land while she feeds and fells trees. The kits also begin to feed on some plants by themselves at this time.

Two kits play by their pond.

The kits are fully weaned by the time they are six weeks old. This means that they no longer need their mother's milk. Yet they will remain in their mother's care for another year, until a new litter of kits is born. She spends much time teaching them. The father beaver helps teach them, too.

The parent beavers in a colony are the ones who fell the trees, do the building, and keep everything repaired. The young beavers help only in emergencies, such as a break in the dam or a flood. They seem to know by instinct what to do, but watching and helping their parents work also helps them learn. This way they will know how to take care of themselves when the time comes for them to leave the home pond for life on their own.

Each spring the mother beaver must prepare for the birth of a new litter of kits. She does this by forcing her mate and their yearlings away from the lodge. As a rule, the father beaver goes to live in one of the refuge holes. The yearlings go to live with him or in some of the other refuge holes. They will return to the lodge when the new litter is about two weeks old. The two-year-old beavers go off on their own at this time.

If the two-year-olds do not leave, their parents force them to go away. If a two-year-old still refuses to go, the parents kill it. This helps prevent overpopulation of the colony. Too many beavers in one colony would quickly use up the supply of food.

Predators

A beaver will often stop its work or play to look around and sniff the air. If it smells danger, it will slap the surface of the water with its tail and then quickly dive to safety. This is the alarm signal to warn other beavers. It can be heard quite far away. Other beavers may pass the warning along as they dive for safety, too.

A beaver will give the alarm signal even when it is on land. A loud "thump" on the ground can often startle the enemy. If it does, the beaver may have time to get away to the safety of the pond.

This beaver has spotted danger and is diving under the water.

A beaver has few natural predators when it is in the water. The otter and large fish might sometimes prey on the smallest kits.

A beaver is in much greater danger on land. Wolves, coyotes, bears, wolverines, cougars, and bobcats all prey on it. The smaller kits may also be attacked by foxes, hawks, and owls. The underwater entrances of the beaver lodge are good defense against most of these land-living predators.

A beaver will fight for its life if it must. It bites attackers with its big front teeth and powerful jaw muscles. A beaver can inflict a terrible wound! If forced to fight, the beaver hisses and grunts loudly. Sometimes it also can be heard sharpening its incisor teeth before the attack.

A kit has to be very careful when on land.

CHAPTER FOUR:

Most people never see a beaver at work. They see only the felled trees and the gnawed-off stumps. An adult beaver can fell a tree five inches (13 cm) thick in about three minutes. There are reports of beavers felling trees four feet (1.23 m) thick! Most of the time, beavers fell smaller trees, perhaps two to eight inches (5-20 cm) thick.

Working in pairs

The beavers are very busy at night. They feed and fell trees. They also trim off all the trees' branches, cut the trunks into logs and haul branches and logs to the water.

As a rule, beavers work in pairs. One beaver does the work while the other stands watch for predators. While gnawing at a tree, a beaver sits on its hind legs and props itself up with its tail. The beaver tilts its head to one side so its sharp incisor teeth can get the best bite. It may even hold onto the tree trunk with its forefeet. The beaver will cut two grooves, one higher up on the tree trunk than the other. Then it chips out the wood left between the two grooves.

Beavers dropped this tree right into the water.

One beaver might gnaw all the way around the trunk of a tree. Another might do its gnawing all on one side.

When the tree starts to fall, both beavers head for the safety of the pond. They wait in the water to make sure the sound of the tree crashing to the ground did not attract any predators. If it did not, they will return to the felled tree to begin the job of cutting it into pieces.

If the trees that beavers fell are close to water, they do not have much trouble getting the wood to the pond. But if they have felled a tree farther back in the forest, the job becomes more difficult. A beaver can carry small sticks and branches in its forefeet or in its mouth. To move larger logs, a beaver may push them with its forefeet or with its nose and the top of its head. A beaver may also back up, pulling the load behind itself. Each log weighs about the same. The beavers cut the tree trunk into longer and longer logs as the thickness of the tree decreases.

A colony of beavers may cut down several thousand trees each year. This provides the beaver with plenty of food to eat. It also keeps his incisors worn down as they grow. It provides the beaver with plenty of wood for building their lodge and dams, too.

Lodges

Some beavers build their lodge on a small island in the water. Others make their own island by piling up mud from the bottom of the river, lake or pond. On top of this foundation they put sticks, twigs, branches, and logs. Then the entire pile is plastered with mud. A beaver packs the mud into place with its forefeet and the side of its head. It does not use its tail, as some people think. Only a small hole in the top of the pile is left open. This lets fresh air enter the lodge and stale air escape.

Then the beavers begin to bite and dig into the pile, starting at the bottom. They always make at least two tunnels as underwater entrances. One will be used to bring branches inside at mealtime. The other will be used by the beavers to come and go. This entrance will always be kept clear in case a quick escape from danger is necessary. At the end of the entrances, in the middle of the pile, the beavers hollow out a room. They make the floor slightly above water level. Then a bed or sleeping shelf is

The pond around this beaver lodge was drained. The underwater entrance can be seen behind the log.

carved out of the pile several inches above the floor. Wood chips on the floor and the sleeping shelf will help keep the beavers dry.

A beaver lodge can be huge. It often stands six or eight feet (1.8-2.4 m) above the water and can be fifteen to twenty feet (4.6-6.1 m) wide. The inside room of a beaver lodge is about eighteen inches (46 cm) high and eight feet (2.4 m) wide. That is big enough for a human being to crawl inside! Newly-paired beavers start with smaller lodges. They make them bigger as their family grows.

A well-built lodge is very strong. No predator can break into a beaver lodge once the mud freezes solid!

Dams

A beaver dam is made of sticks, stones and anything else a beaver might find. Old railroad ties and deer antlers have been found in beaver dams. So has an old television antenna! Beavers have used cornstalks for their dams when no wood was nearby.

Beaver dams come in all shapes and sizes. Some may be very sloppy and others very finely made. Most dams take advantage of any natural anchor already in the water. It may be a big rock, a stump or a tree. This is why many beaver dams zig-zag in odd lines. Dams may be bowed upstream, against the current. This lessens the water pressure against them and helps prevent them from breaking.

Most beaver dams are about five feet (1.5 m) high and several hundred feet long. Large dams are often many years old. They may have been added to by generations of beavers. A dam in Montana that reaches 2,140 feet (653 m) is thought to be the longest. Another dam, in Wyoming, is eighteen feet high (5.5 m).

To build a dam, beavers start at the bottom in much the same way as they built their lodge. First they force branches and twigs into the mud. They weight them down with stones so that they do not float away. Then they add more layers of branches, twigs, logs and other debris. Each layer is woven into the one before it so that the dam will hold together. Finally the beavers plaster the upstream side of the dam with leaves, debris and more mud, patting it all in place with their forefeet.

The upstream side of a beaver dam is usually straight up and down. The downstream side slopes at an angle. This makes the dams wider at the base than at the top. They may be as much as ten feet (3.1 m) wide at the base.

Older beaver dams are strong enough to walk across. They may become a regular bridge across a stream or pond for many forest animals. Plants often grow on top of a beaver dam. Their roots help to strengthen it. Silt and leaves flowing down the stream get stuck in the upstream side of the dam and help strengthen it, too.

No matter how big or how strong the beavers make their dam, they often must make repairs. The main problem is leaks. These they plug with leaves, debris and mud.

In times of high water, the beavers may have to cut a spillway. Spillways are cuts in the top of the dam that can safely carry away extra water so that it does not break the dam. The beavers may also dig a small ditch around the side of the dam. This lets extra water safely flow out over the bare ground nearby. The beavers will also work to raise the top of the dam

This winter scene shows a beaver dam that crosses a stream.

and to lengthen it. By doing this, the dam can safely back up more water and make a bigger, deeper pond.

Beavers will often build smaller dams downstream to back up water against the main dam. This evens

This drawing shows a cross-section of a dam (left), a food cache (center), and a lodge (right).

the water pressure against the main dam and helps prevent it from breaking. Smaller dams are often built upstream, too. These flood more of the forest, so the beavers can reach more food trees.

Canals

Building dams and a lodge takes a lot of wood. To fell enough trees, the beavers may have to go quite far back into the forest. They build canals so that they can get their wood back to the pond more easily and safely.

Some beaver canals go hundreds of feet out from the home pond. They may be two or three feet (62-92 cm) deep and just as wide. If the ground slopes up from the pond, the beavers build their canals in short sections at different levels like steps. Each section is connected to the next by a small dam called a lock. These locks are made of dirt piled two to four feet (62-123 cm) high. They back up ground water and runoff water from rains and melting snows, filling each section of the canal. Each lock has a slope on its downhill side. A beaver slides its load of wood over these locks when going from one section of the canal to the next until it gets to the pond.

After all this work, the beaver family likes to stay in one place as long as it can. One lodge in Wyoming is said to have been in constant use for more than thirty years.

Still, the time may come when all of the food trees in the nearby forest have been felled. Then the beavers are forced to find a new place to live.

CHAPTER FIVE:
Controls are needed

Few animals change the land where they live as much as the beaver. Beavers can do a lot of good, but they can also do a lot of damage.

In the right place, the dams beavers build help conserve water and prevent floods. They also help stop erosion by stopping good soil from being swept

Beavers caused flooding by building their dam along this country road.

out to sea. The ponds that form behind the beaver dams also help many kinds of wildlife survive.

In the wrong place, beaver dams may flood croplands and pastures, highways and railroad tracks. This flooding can cause millions of dollars worth of damage. It can also kill many valuable trees. Beavers can ruin an orchard, a tree farm, or a nursery. More than one beaver has been known to fell a tree that crushed a roof of a building!

When these things happen, landowners start calling the beavers pests. They will try all sorts of ways to get rid of the beavers and their dams. They may even dynamite the dams! But most of the time beavers just work harder than ever the next night to repair the damage. They may even build their dam higher! Beavers can be very stubborn animals.

The only way to solve the problem may be to move the beaver and its family to a place where their building projects will not bother people. This is often one of the jobs of the government game departments. Landowners cannot simply set a trap and kill the beaver that is causing trouble. Most of the time that would be against the law.

Beaver trapping is allowed today only during certain times of the year called trapping seasons. The law also sets limits as to how many beavers each trapper can take in one season. These seasons and limits change from place to place according to how many beavers there are each year in each area.

Beavers are trapped for their beautiful fur.

There are some people today who still earn their living trapping beavers and other fur-bearing animals. These trappers who sell fur for profit must be licensed. Beaver fur is still in demand, and so is the beavers' castoreum. The fur is not used for hats as much now, but it still is used for coats and trimmings on clothing. The castoreum is no longer used for medicine, but is used as a base for perfume.

The number of beavers can now be controlled. This is one of the many jobs of a wildlife manager. Wise laws and good managers can help prevent the beaver from overpopulating the woods and damaging private property. They can also help prevent the beaver from ever becoming extinct in North America.

MAP:

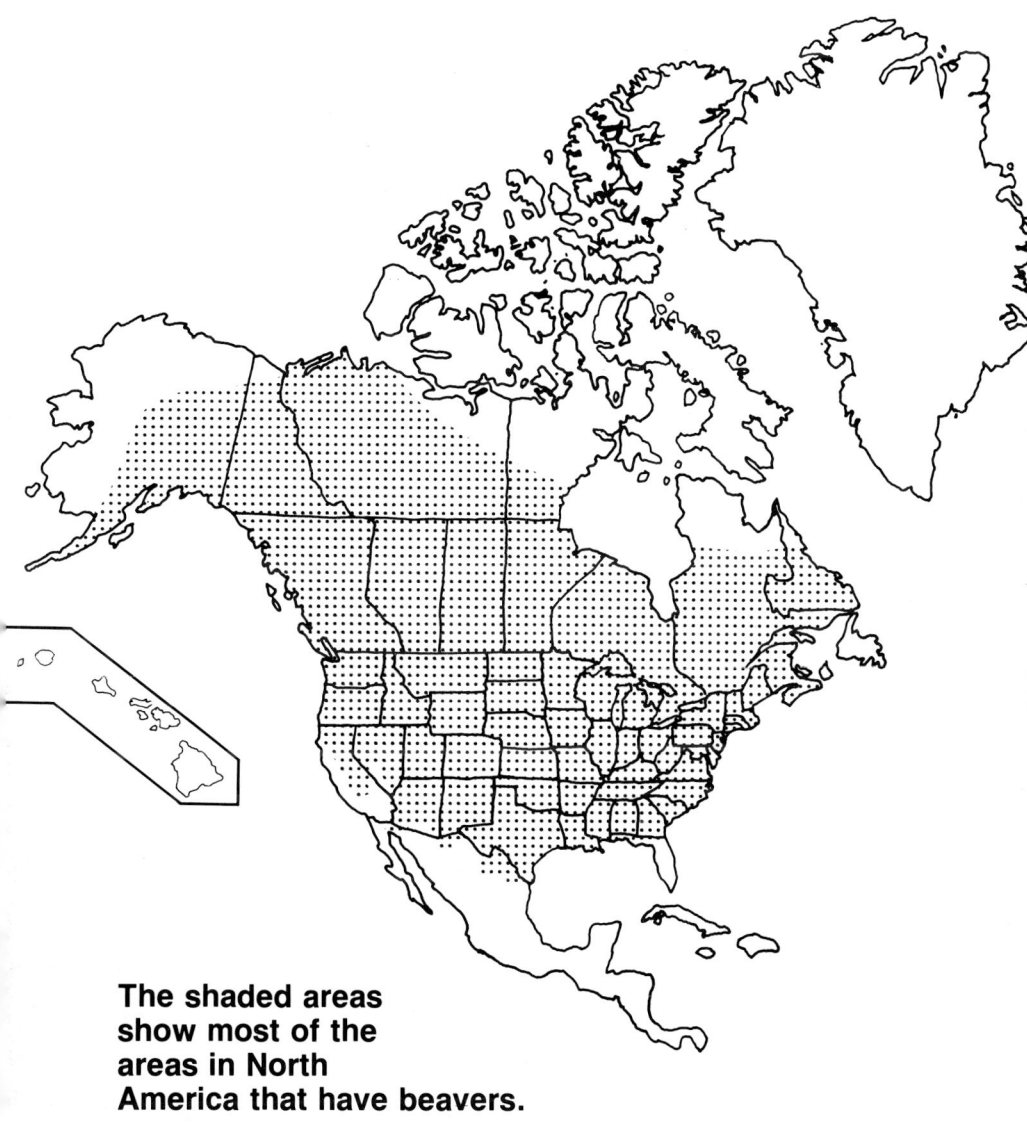

The shaded areas show most of the areas in North America that have beavers.

INDEX/GLOSSARY:

BABIES 26, 27

BURROW 8, 19, 20, 23 — *A hole dug in the ground by an animal.*

CACHE 23, 25, 38 — *A place where food is stored.*

CAMBIUM 21, 22 — *The soft inner bark of a tree between the outside bark and the inner wood from which new bark and wood develop.*

CAPYBARA 4 — *The largest rodent in the world, up to four feet long and weighing over 100 pounds.*

CASTORS 11 — *Two organs in the beaver's body at the base of its tail that discharge an oil called castoreum.*

CASTOREUM 11, 17, 25, 44 — *An oil discharged by the beaver's castor glands and used to waterproof its fur.*

CHEEK TEETH 12 — *Four teeth in the back of the beaver's mouth on either side, top and bottom that are used for grinding the food it eats.*

COLONY 18, 21, 25, 26, 28, 33 — *A group of beavers who live in a certain place.*

CREPUSCULAR 8 — *Active during the twilight of dawn and dusk.*

DAMS 35

DEBRIS 36, 37 — *Things that have been discarded, by nature or by human beings.*

DIET 21

ECTOPARASITE 11 — *A parasite that lives on the outer surface of an animal (a parasite is an animal that lives off another animal).*

FUR 7, 11

GESTATION 26 — *The period of time before birth that a mother carries her young inside her body.*

HABITAT 18-20 — *The region a plant or animal naturally is found.*

HERBIVOROUS 21 — *Feeding on grass or plants.*

HIBERNATE 8 — *To spend the winter sleeping.*

INCISOR 12, 15, 26, 30, 31, 33 *A front tooth used for cutting.*

INSTINCT 28 — *A tendency that an animal has when it is born to behave in a way special to that species.*

KIT 21, 26-28, 30 — *A young beaver.*

LOCK 40 — *A wall that divides a waterway into lower and upper levels.*

LODGES 8, 19-23, 30, 33, 35, 36, 40 — *The homes of beavers.*

MATING 25, 26

MONOGAMOUS 26 — *Having only one mate at a time.*

NOCTURNAL 8 — *Active at night.*

PELT 7 — *An animal skin, especially with the fur or hair still on it.*

PHYSICAL CHARACTERISTICS 4, 9, 11

PREDATORS 16, 29-32, 35 — *Animals that hunt and kill other animals (called prey) for food.*

PREY 30 — *An animal hunted and killed for food by another animal.*

RANGE 45

REFUGE HOLES 19, 20, 24, 28

RODENT 4, 8, 9, 12 — *A mammal that has ever-growing front teeth for gnawing.*

SAPLING 22 — *A young tree.*

SCENT GLAND 11 — *An organ in an animal's body that discharges a substance that has an odor unique to that animal.*

TAIL 13

TEETH 12

TRAPPING 7, 42

TUNDRA 17 — *A vast, nearly level, treeless plain in the artic region.*

WEBBING 10 — *A membrane connecting the toes of an animal.*

READ AND ENJOY THE SERIES:

- THE WHITETAIL
- THE PHEASANT
- THE BALD EAGLE
- THE WOLVES
- THE SQUIRRELS
- THE BEAVER
- THE GRIZZLY
- THE MALLARD
- THE RACCOON
- THE WILD CATS
- THE RATTLESNAKE
- THE SHEEP
- THE ALLIGATOR
- THE CARIBOU
- THE CANADA GOOSE
- THE FOXES

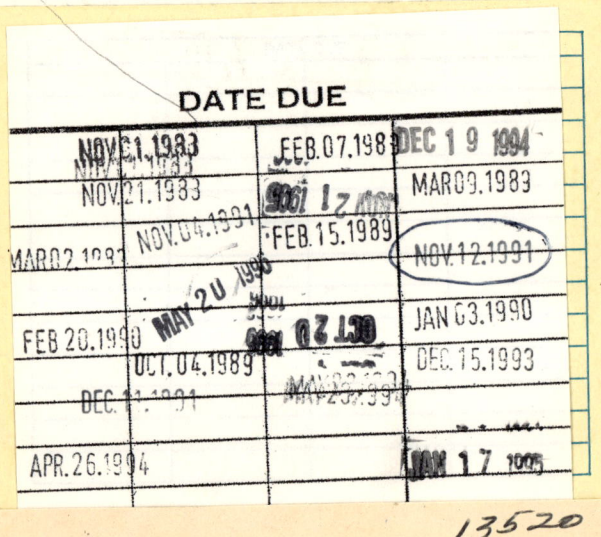

13520

599.32   Nentl, Jerolyn Ann.
N   The beaver.